Pi Faitau
The Samoan Alphabet

Aa Ee Ii

Luisa Auva'a Tupou

Dedication

Mo le matai a si o matou aiga o Lua'ilelupe Fa'alafua Auva'a ma le masiofo o Rita Hunt Auva'a fa'afetai tele lava mo lua alofa, fa'atuatua, ma fesoasoaniga e fa'atinoina lenei sini.

To my boys Joe, Henele and Sale thank you for awakening the stories of my heart and instilling bravery in me to share.

Note

H, K, R, are three letters introduced to accommodate use of foreign words such as English, Greek, and Latin.

'Alāfau
Cheek

'Apu
Apple

'Ā'ā

Alofa
Love

'Ato
Basket

'Elefane
Elephant

Esi
Papaya

‘Ē‘ē

'Eli
Dig

'Ēlei
Patterned Barkcloth

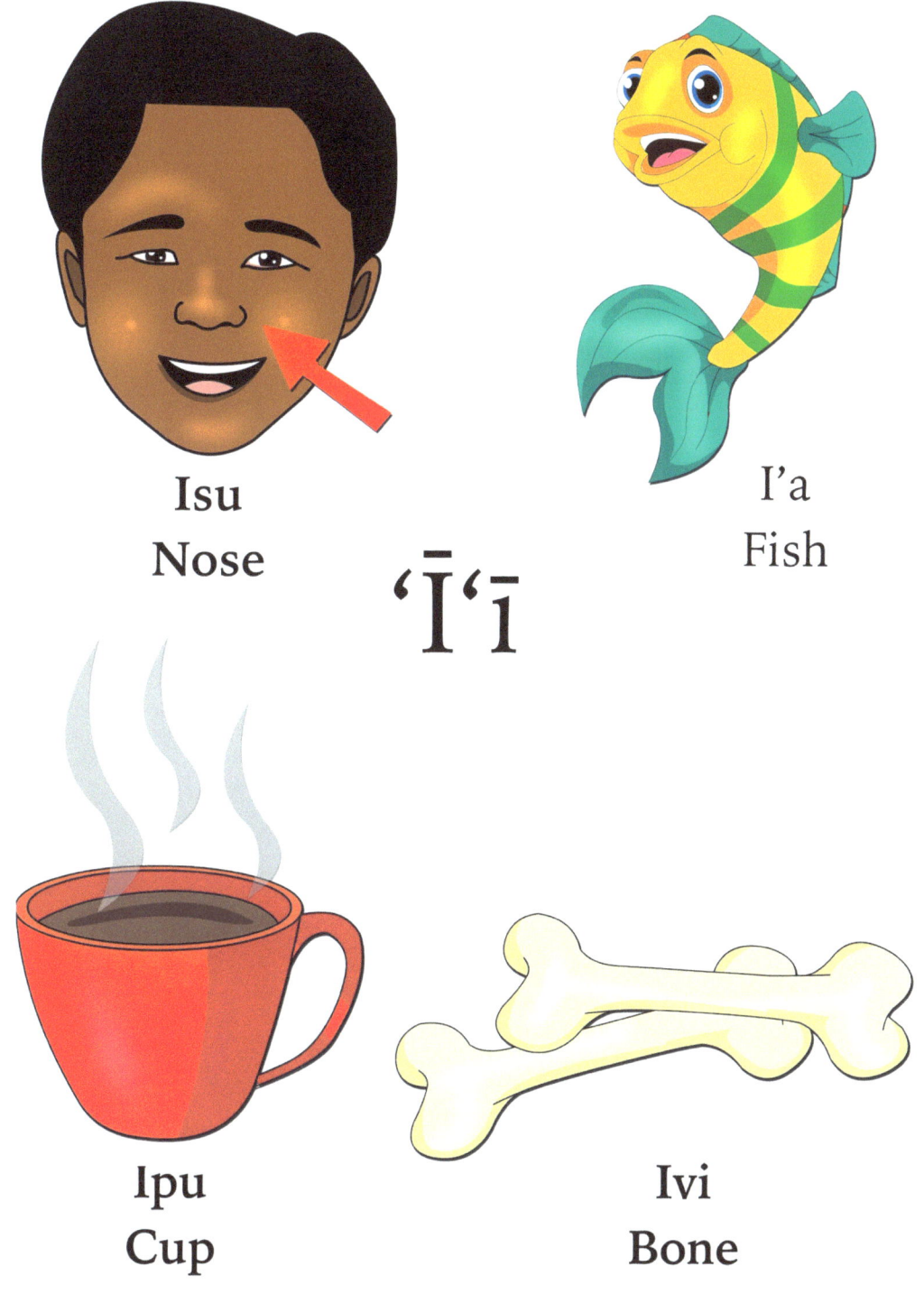

Isu
Nose

I'a
Fish

ʻĪʻī

Ipu
Cup

Ivi
Bone

Ula
Flower Neckalace

Uati
Clock

ʻŪʻū

Uila
Bicycle

Ulo
Pot

Fala
Pineapple

Fu'a
Flag

Ff

Fagu
Bottle

Fale
House

Gata
Snake

Gutu
Mouth

Gg

Ga'oi
Thief

Galu
Wave

Logo
Bell

La'au
Tree

Ll

Lole
Candy

Laumei
Turtle

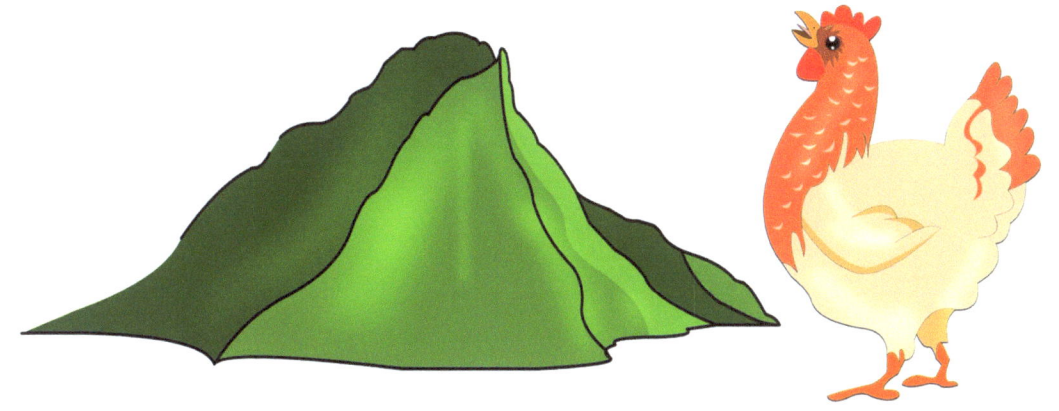

Mauga
Mountain

Moa
Chicken

Mm

Musika
Music

Maile
Dog

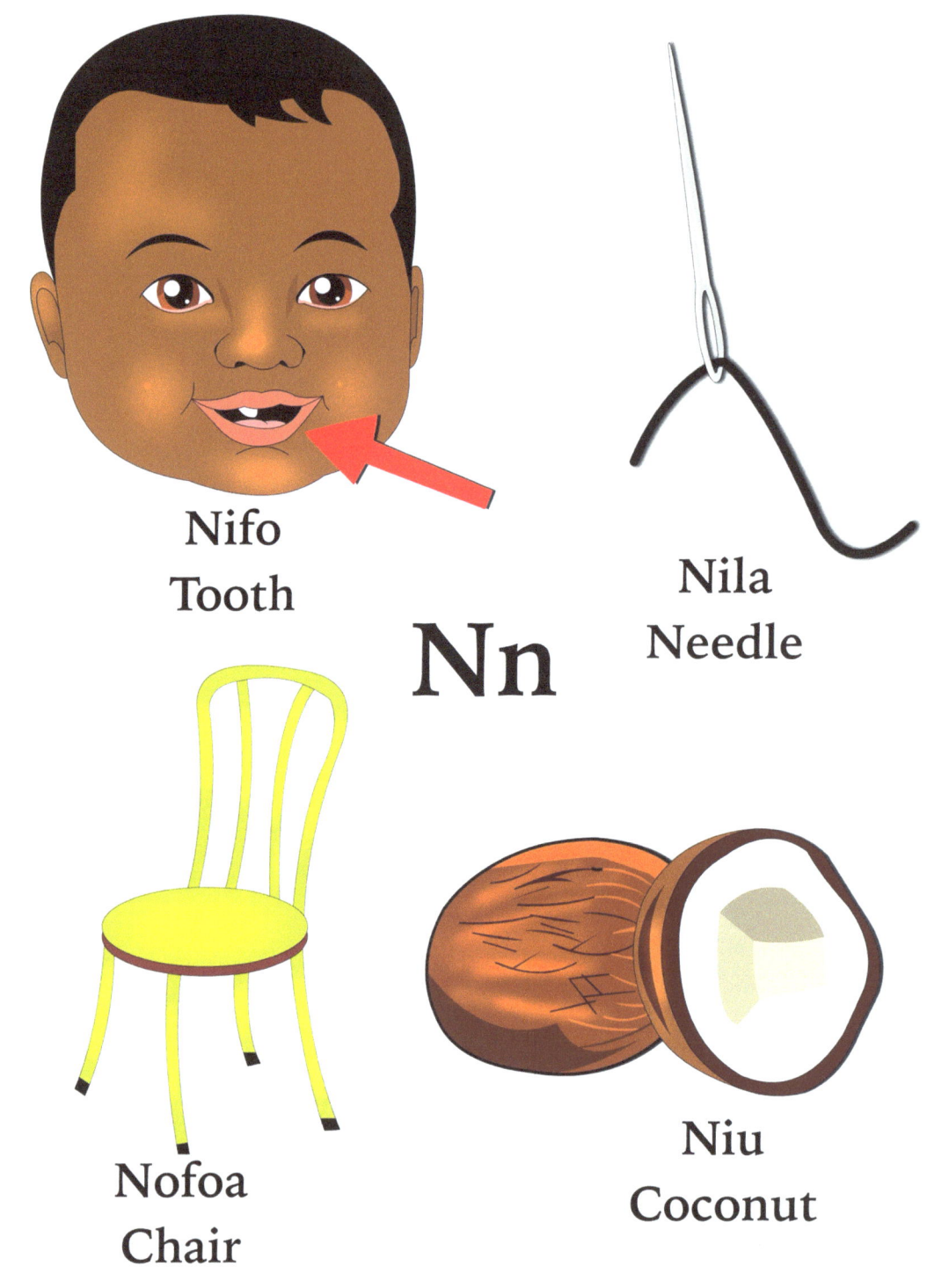

Nifo — Tooth

Nila — Needle

Nn

Nofoa — Chair

Niu — Coconut

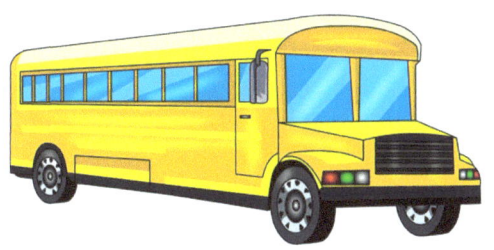

Pasi
Bus

Polo
Ball

Pp

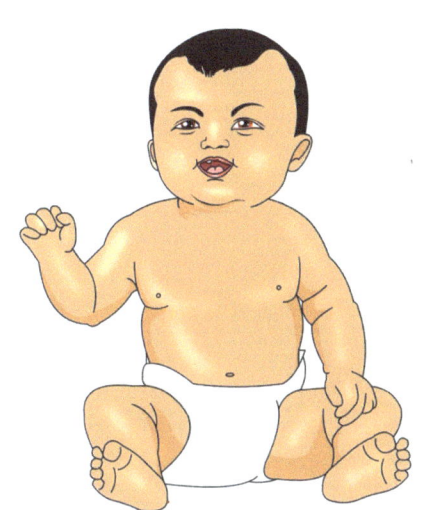

Pepe
Baby

Paluni
Balloon

Sisi
Cheese

Savali
Walk

Ss

Solofonua
Horse

Sei
Flower

Tusi
Book

Ta'avale
Car

Tt

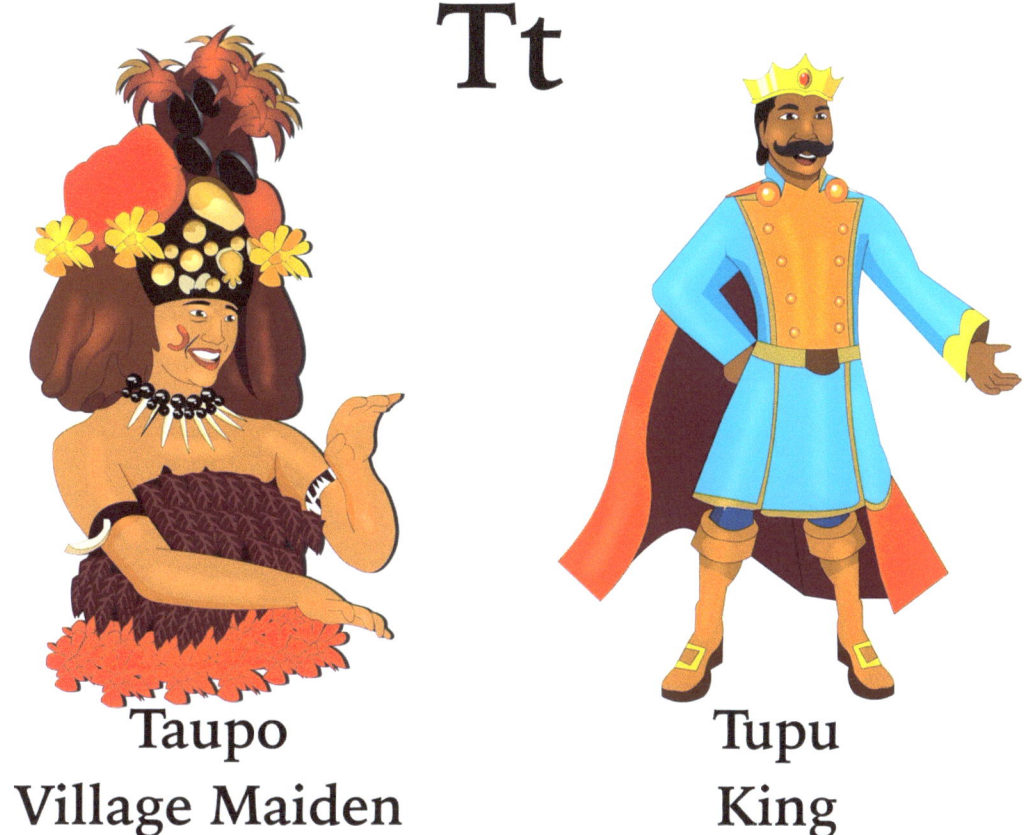

Taupo
Village Maiden

Tupu
King

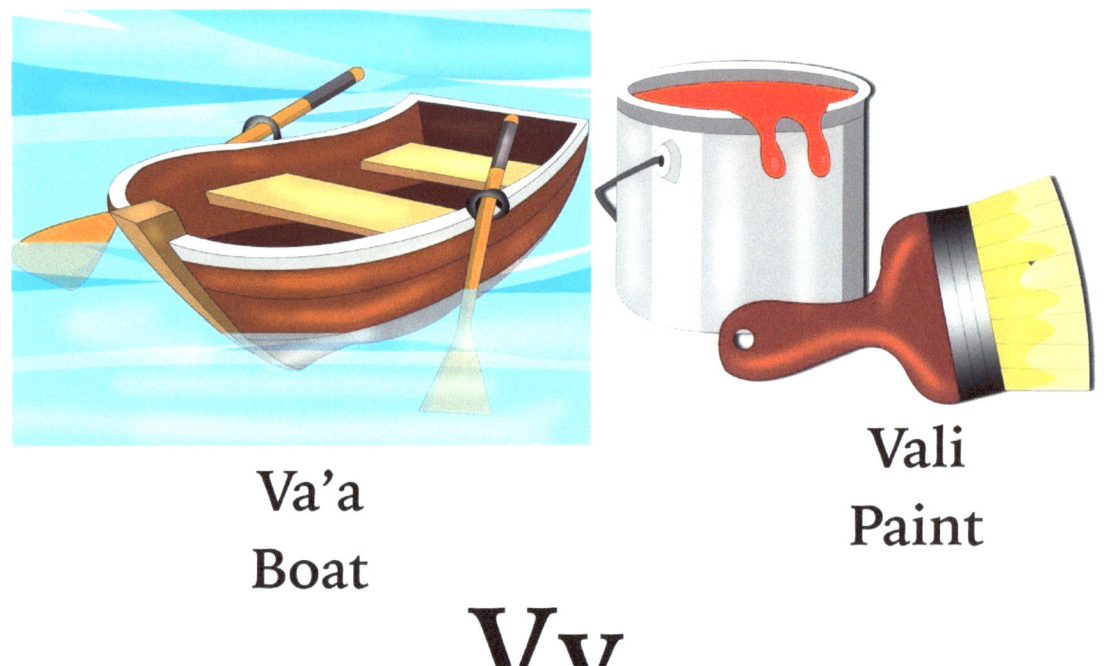

Va'a
Boat

Vali
Paint

Vv

Va'alele
Plane

Vai
Water

Herota
Herod

Hh

Helikopa
Helicopter

Kk

Kirikiti
Cricket

Keke
Cake

Rosa
Rose

Rr

Rapiti
Rabit

CPSIA information can be obtained
at www.ICGtesting.com
Printed in the USA
LVHW072317130519
617742LV00002B/8/P